SMILE-A-WHILE

ANIMAL JOKES

By Gary Chmielewski
Drawings by Ron G. Clark

© 1986 Rourke Enterprises, Inc.

All rights reserved. No part of this book may be reproduced or utilized in any form or by any means, electronic or mechanical including photocopying, recording or by any information storage and retrieval system without permission in writing from the publisher.

Library of Congress Cataloging in Publication Data

Chmielewski, Gary, 1946-
  Animals.

  (Smile-a-while joke book)
  Summary: An illustrated collection of jokes and riddles about animals, such as "Which dog always knows what time it is? A watch dog."
  1. Animals—Juvenile humor. 2. Wit and humor, Juvenile. 3. Riddles, Juvenile. [1. Animals—Wit and humor. 2. Jokes. 3. Riddles] I. Title. II. Series.
PN6231.A5C46 1986   818'.5402   86-17684
ISBN 0-86592-687-5

ROURKE ENTERPRISES, INC.
VERO BEACH, FLORIDA 32964

What animals do you find at every baseball game?
BATS!

What does a skunk do when it's angry?
It raises a stink!

A donkey seeing a zebra for the first time said to himself "Imagine that! A donkey that's been to jail!"

What do bees do with their honey?
They cell it.

What animal eats with its tail?
They all do. No animal removes its tail to eat!

Which dog always know what time it is?
A watch dog!

What is cow hide used for?
To hold the cow together!

First Hunter: I just ran into a big bear!
Second Hunter: Did you let him have both barrels?
First Hunter: Both barrels — I let him have the whole gun!

Jimmy: I went swimming today and a fish bit off one of my fingers.
Tommy: Which one?
Jimmy: I don't know. All fish look alike.

What did one fish say to the other fish after it was hooked?
"That's what you get for not keeping your mouth shut!"

What do dogs and trees have in common?
Their bark!

What did one firefly say to the other firefly?
Your son sure is bright for his age!

Jack: Your dog just bit my ankle.
Mary: What did you expect? He's just a small dog and c[an't reach] any higher!

What fish goes well with peanut butter in your sandwich?
A jelly fish!

What kind of cat hangs around a bowling alley?
An alley cat!

What kind of dog hands out tickets?
A police dog!

Why did the elephant quit the circus?
He didn't want to work for peanuts anymore!

Which fish go to heaven when they die?
Angel fish!

Why did the farmer put bells on his cows?
The horns didn't work!

Why are cats larger at night than in the day?
Because they're let out at night and taken in in the morning!

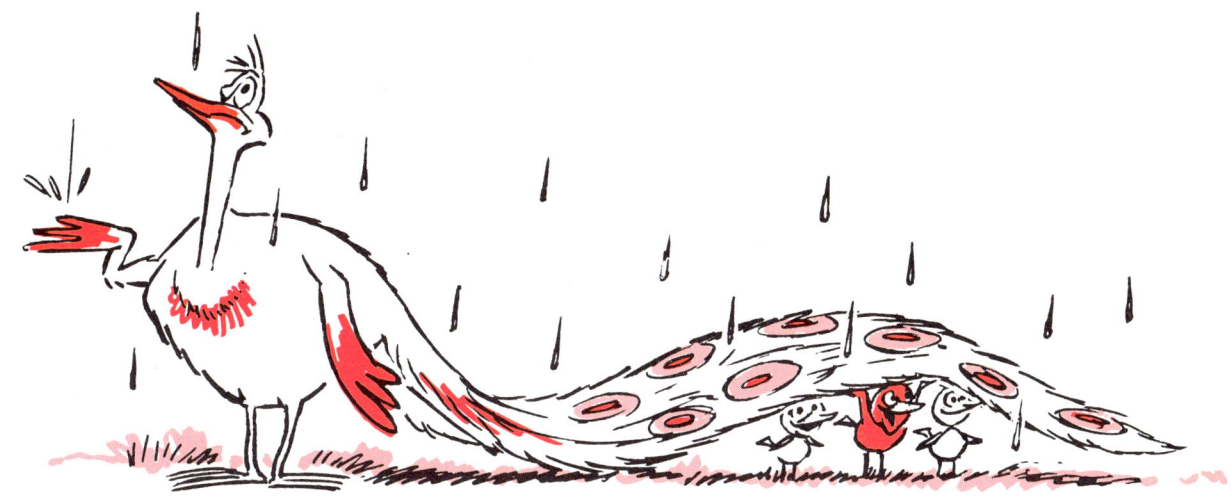

Did you hear the story about the peacock?
No
Well, it's a beautiful tale!

What kind of dog can be found at a bowling alley?
A setter!

Gail: I got a cow for my birthday.
Tom: Does it give milk?
Gail: No, I have to take it from her.

What kind of sharks never eat women?
Man-eating sharks!

Why do ducks dive?
They want to liquidate their bills!

A young man was helping a farmer herd some cattle when the farmer asked him to hold the bull for a moment.
"No sir," said the young man. "I don't mind being a director in this operation, but I don't want to be a stockholder!"

Little Girl: How much are those puppies in the window?
Pet Store Owner: Twenty dollars a piece.
Little Girl: How much is a whole one?

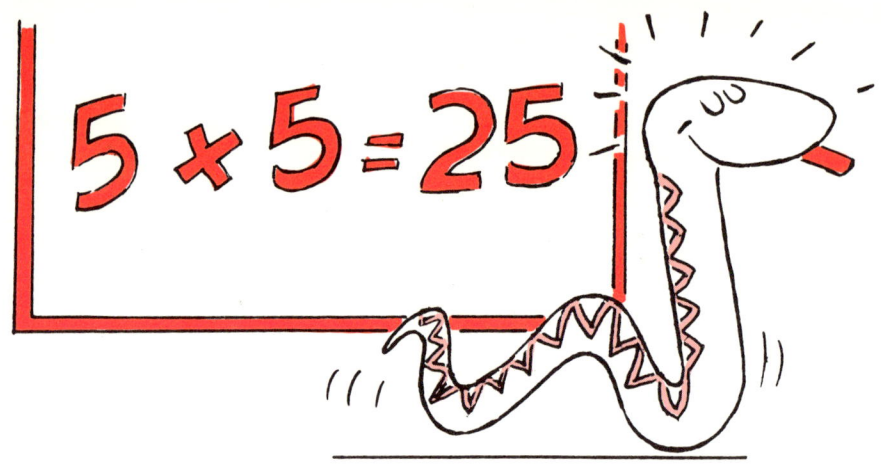

What kind of snake is very good at maths?
An adder.

Crockett: I've got an alligator on my boat named Ginger.
Tubbs: Does Ginger bite?
Crockett: No, Ginger snaps!

Bobby: I've got a cat who can say his own name.
Charlie: That's great! What's your cat's name?
Bobby: "Meow"!

Julie: My dog Chewbacca is sick, so we're taking him to an animal doctor.
Stevie: Gee, I thought all doctors were people.

What should you do when a bull charges you?
Pay him!

Charles: My parents bought me a bird for my birthday.
Rita: What kind?
Charles: A keet.
Rita: You mean a parakeet.
Charles: No, they only bought me one!

What did the baby chicken say when it saw an orange in the mother's nest?
Look at the orange Mama laid!

Veterinarian: Has your dog ever have fleas?
Little Boy: No, only puppies!

Belinda: We have a new dog.
George: What's he like?
Belinda: Anything we feed him!

Nancy: How do you get down off an elephant?
Robert: You climb down.
Nancy: WRONG!
Robert: You grease his sides and slide down.
Nancy: WRONG!
Robert: You get a ladder and climb down.
Nancy: WRONG! You can't get down off an elephant. You get it off a goose!

What did the man say when his dog ran away?
Doggone-it!

Mother tiger to baby tiger: What are you doing?
Baby tiger: I'm chasing a hunter around the tree.
Mother tiger: How often do I have to tell you not to play with your food!

What' a fighter's favorite dog?
A boxer!

What kind of snake snaps at people?
A garter snake!

What do you call a cat who drinks lemonade?
A sour puss!

How many legs does a mule have if you call a tail a leg?
Four – calling a tail a leg doesn't make it a leg.

What did the elephant say when he sat on the box of cookies?
That's the way the cookies crumble!

What is a boxer's favorite bird?
A duck!

DATE DUE

FEB 28 '90		
APR 30 '90		
ILL 6-8-91		
JY 27 '91		
APR 6 '9?		
MR 8 '93		
MR 31 '93		
FEB 24		
MAR 18		
MAR 18 1997		
DEC 4 1997		
NOV 21 '01		
GAYLORD		PRINTED IN U.S.A.